DENESULINE

Carol Koopmans

Published by Weigl Educational Publishers Limited
6325 10th Street S.E.
Calgary, Alberta, Canada T2H 2Z9

Website: www.weigl.com

Library and Archives Canada Cataloguing in Publication
Koopmans, Carol
Denesuline / author: Carol Koopmans ; editor: Heather Kissock.
(Aboriginal peoples of Canada)
Includes index.
Also available in electronic format.
ISBN 978-1-55388-649-5 (bound).--ISBN 978-1-55388-655-6 (pbk.)
1. Chipewyan Indians--Juvenile literature. I. Kissock, Heather
II. Title. III. Series: Aboriginal peoples of Canada (Calgary, Alta.)

E99.C59K662 2010 j971.004'972 C2009-907313-7

Printed in the United States of America in Mankato, Minnesota
1 2 3 4 5 6 7 8 9 14 13 12 11 10

062010
WEP230610

Photograph and Text Credits
Cover: Canadian Museum of Civilization (VI-D-24,a, b, D2003-11565); Canadian Museum of Civilization: pages 8B (VI-Z-244, D2005-21229), 9T (VI-D-257, D2004-07091), 15B (VI-D-106 a, b, D2003-11526), 21B (VI-D-35, D2003-08641), 23 (VI-D-106 a, b, D2003-11526); Getty Images: pages 5, 7, 10, 11, 14, 21T; McCord Museum: pages 8T, 9M, 9B, 12B, 13B; NWT Archives: pages 4, 6, 12T, 13T, 15T, 16, 17, 20.

We gratefully acknowledge the financial support of the Government of Canada through the Canada Book Fund for our publishing activities.

PROJECT COORDINATOR Heather Kissock
DESIGN Terry Paulhus
ILLUSTRATOR Martha Jablonski-Jones

Contents

The Denesuline are one of Canada's **First Nations**. Their **traditional** lands are located in Canada's subarctic. This is an area that covers the northern parts of Canada from Labrador to British Columbia.

Much of the subarctic is barren, nearly flat land called tundra. Summers are short, and winters are cold. The Denesuline's survival has depended on their ability to live in this environment.

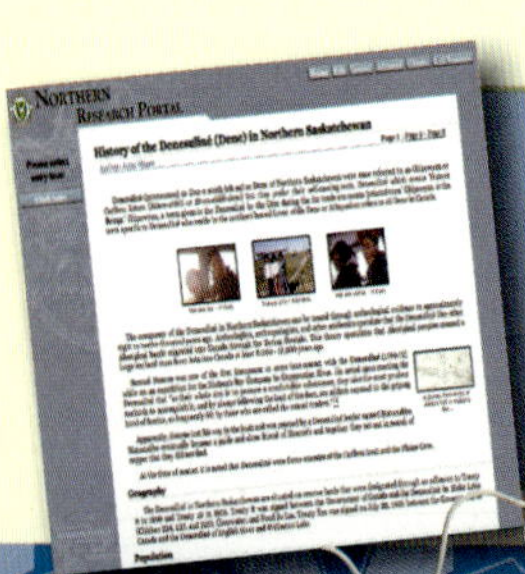

NET LINK

Learn what other names the Denesuline are known by at **http://scaa.usask.ca/gallery/northern/content?pg=ex04-1**.

Denesuline Homes

TEEPEES

In the past, the Denesuline lived in teepees during the summer months. Teepees were cone-shaped buildings. They were built using animal skins that were stretched over tree poles. The skins could be rolled up to allow cool breezes to flow in and out.

Denesuline Ideas

The Denesuline built ridge-pole lodges to live in on short hunting trips. The lodges had a pole frame that looked like an upside-down "V." Fur, bark, or leaves covered the frame.

WIGWAMS

The Denesuline used wigwams as their winter homes. Wigwams had a dome-shaped frame made from long, thin poles. Bark, animal furs, or mats of leaves were used to cover the frame.

Denesuline Clothing

MEN'S CLOTHING

In the past, Denesuline men wore pants or leggings and a long-sleeved shirt. Men's shirts had a pointed shirt tail on the front and back.

WOMEN'S CLOTHING

Women's clothing was similar to men's. Women wore pants along with long-sleeved tops. Sometimes, they wore skirts instead of pants.

PARKAS

Men and women wore parkas to keep warm in the winter months. Parkas were often made from moose or caribou fur. Women's parkas had extra room in the back to allow for carrying a child.

MITTENS

Mittens kept hands warm in cold weather. The Denesuline made their mittens using animal skins and furs.

MOCCASINS

The Denesuline wore moccasins on their feet. The moccasins were often made from moose skin because of its strength.

Hunting and Gathering

CARIBOU

The Denesuline relied heavily on the caribou that roam Canada's subarctic. Their meat was eaten fresh or dried into **pemmican**.

BEAR

Bears are also found throughout the forests and woodlands of the subarctic. The Denesuline often put bear meat in stews.

BEAVER

The Denesuline also hunted small animals, such as beaver. Their meat could be cooked immediately or dried for future use.

Finding food was the responsibility of both men and women. Men hunted for game and fished in nearby waters. Women picked berries when in season. They also prepared food for winter storage.

RABBIT

The Denesuline often set traps to catch rabbits. Once caught, rabbit meat was cooked on its own or put in stews.

FISH

Nets made from raw caribou skin or bark were cast in streams to catch fish. Trout and pike were two types of fish the Denesuline caught.

BERRIES

Huckleberries were important to the Denesuline diet. They were used in pemmican, dried for later use, or mashed to make juice.

Denesuline Tools

BASIC TOOLS

Tools made from stone, bone, and wood helped people complete tasks in their daily life. Denesuline men used tools such as axes, spears, and knives.

Denesuline Ideas

The Denesuline braided strips of caribou hide to make fishing nets and bags.

UTENSILS

Women's tools included spoons and ladles for handling food. These **utensils** were made from wood and animal horns. Bones were often made into scrapers for **tanning** hides.

Moving from Place to Place

CANOES

Water travel was done by canoe. Denesuline canoes could be made from spruce or birchbark. Sometimes, the Denesuline made larger boats. To do this, they stretched moose skins over spruce frames.

Denesuline Ideas

The Denesuline often relied on dogs to help them travel. In winter, dogsleds were used to carry people and animals on hunting trips.

SNOWSHOES

When travelling over land, the Denesuline often went by foot. In winter, they would use snowshoes to help them walk across deep snow. Snowshoes stopped them from sinking in snow.

Denesuline Music and Dance

Drums were an important part of Denesuline music. They were used to accompany singing and dancing. Drummers were usually men. They held the drum in one hand and hit it with a **mallet**.

Denesuline Ideas

Sometimes, men sit around one big drum. They strike the drum together with their mallets.

Drums were made of animal hide, normally caribou, that was stretched onto a round, wooden frame. Before it was placed on the frame, the hide was softened over an open fire. This gave the drum the right sound.

NET LINK

Find out more about Dene drums at **www.kayas.ca/denedrum.html**.

The Sun Taken in a Snare

A long time ago, a brother and sister lived together on their own. They survived by hunting and fishing. Every day, they would check their **snares** to see if they had caught any animals.

Over time, they noticed that the days were becoming shorter and the weather was getting colder. The Sun rarely appeared in the sky. They knew that, if this continued, the world would freeze and Earth's creatures would not survive. They knew they had to try to save Earth's creatures.

One day, the sister was checking her snares. She noticed that the Sun was caught in one of the snares and was slowly dying. She ran to get her brother. When he returned, they both approached the Sun. The Sun begged for its life. If they let it go, the Sun promised to go back to the sky and shine down on Earth and its creatures.

The brother and sister agreed to this deal. Ever since, the Sun has shone down on Earth.

Denesuline Art

The Denesuline expressed themselves through many forms of art. Women would decorate their clothing using porcupine quills. They used dyes from plants to colour the quills. They then wove the coloured quills onto their clothing in interesting patterns.

Denesuline Ideas

Once a basket was put together, colourful designs were added using dyes made from berries or roots.

Baskets made from woven spruce roots were common in Denesuline homes. Some baskets were also made from birchbark. Spruce roots were used to sew the pieces together.

Make a Drum and Mallet

Materials

2 balloons
1 embroidery ring or other circular frame
2 elastic bands
1 piece of cloth
1 stick or branch (1.25 centimetres in diameter, and 30 centimetres long)
Paints for decorating

1. Cut the bottom off one of the balloons.
2. Stretch the balloon over the top of the frame. Secure it with an elastic band.
3. Decorate the drum using the paints.
4. Cut the bottom off the other balloon. Stuff the cloth into the end of the balloon to make a small ball.
5. Place the end of the stick in the stuffed balloon. Gather the ends of the balloon around the stick, and fasten them with the other elastic band.
6. Now, your drum and mallet are ready to make music.

Glossary

First Nations: members of Canada's Aboriginal community who are not Inuit or Métis

mallet: a light hammer with a rounded head

pemmican: a mixture of dried meat and berries that has been pounded into powder and mixed with fat

snares: traps used to capture animals

tanning: the process of making leather

traditional: based on the ways of others who have lived before

utensils: kitchen tools

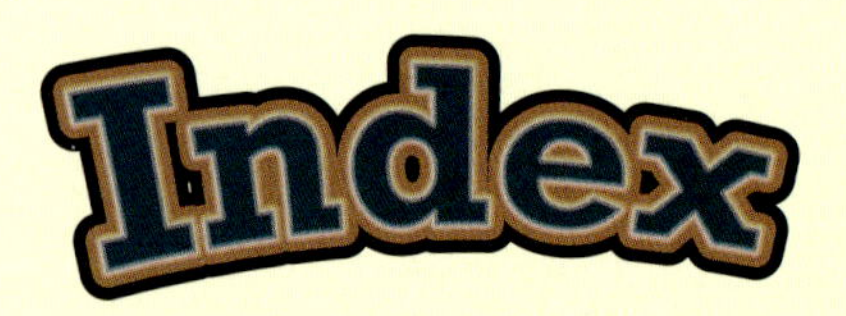

Index